EA

LOCAL-

LONDON

London England Food Guide

Clare F J Caddick

CZYK Publishing Since 2011.

Eat Like a Local

Lock Haven, PA
ISBN: 9781070115450

BOOK DESCRIPTION

Are you excited about planning your next trip?
Do you want an edible experience?
Would you like some culinary guidance from a local?

If you answered yes to any of these questions, then this Eat Like a Local book is for you.

Eat Like A Local –London by author Clare F J Caddick, will offer the inside scoop on the best places to eat in the London England area. Culinary tourism is an import aspect of any travel experience. Food has the ability to tell you a story of a destination, its landscapes, and culture on a single plate. Most food guides tell you how to eat like a tourist. Although there is nothing wrong with that, as part of the Eat Like a Local series, this book will give you a food guide from someone who has lived at your next culinary destination.

In these pages, you will discover advice on having a unique edible experience. This book will not tell you exact addresses or hours but instead will give you excitement and knowledge of food and drinks from a local that you may not find in other travel food guides.

Eat like a local. Slow down, stay in one place, and get to know the food, people, and culture. By the time you finish this book, you will be eager and prepared to travel to your next culinary destination.

OUR STORY

Traveling has always been a passion of the creator of the Eat Like a Local book series. During Lisa's travels in Malta, instead of tasting what the city offered, she ate at a large fast-food chain. However, she realized that her traveling experience would have been more fulfilling if she had experienced the best of local cuisines. Most would agree that food is one of the most important aspects of a culture. Through her travels, Lisa learned how much locals had to share with tourists, especially about food. Lisa created the Eat Like a Local book series to help connect people with locals which she discovered is a topic that locals are very passionate about sharing. So please join me and: Eat, drink, and explore like a local.

TABLE OF CONTENTS

DEDICATION

I dedicate this book to my Nan, Janet. She taught me that what matters is now; she gave me the courage to chase the dream, to see the world, and to eat the cake. She is forever in my heart and in my words. No matter where I live, she will always be my home.

ABOUT THE AUTHOR

Clare is a writer, a traveler and a foodie. Originally from Liverpool, she moved to London at the tender age of twenty one to study Creative and Professional Writing at The University of East London. Having been in London for over ten years now, it's safe to say that despite her strongly remaining Northern accent, she has earned her title of 'Londoner'.

Clare enjoys reading, keeping fit, and then ruining it with masses amount of food and drink. Mostly, Clare loves taking trips overseas. Having travelled to over fifty countries across five continents, Clare loves to be immersed in other cultures, and to see and experience other walks of life. She believes that shared experiences particularly with strangers or those totally different to us are often the most enriching. She loves to chase the sun and feels as connected to the Earth as she did to her Nan. Whether it is mountains or oceans, cities or deserts, sunshine or snowfall, Clare is open-minded about all kinds of exploration, simply basking in her appreciation for any new experiences.

Having returned home from a twenty-six country solo travel stint in 2017, Clare writes freelance travel pieces to keep the adventures alive, whilst of course planning more adventures…

HOW TO USE THIS BOOK

The goal of this book is to help culinary travelers either dream or experience different edible experiences by providing opinions from a local. The author has made suggestions based on their own knowledge. Please do your own research before traveling to the area in case the suggested locations are unavailable.

Travel Advisories: As a first step in planning any trip abroad, check the Travel Advisories for your intended destination.
https://travel.state.gov/content/travel/en/traveladvisories/traveladvisories.html

FROM THE PUBLISHER

Traveling can be one of the most important parts of a person's life. The anticipation and memories that you have are some of the best. As a publisher of the *Eat Like a Local*, Greater Than a Tourist, as well as the popular *50 Things to Know* book series, we strive to help you learn about new places, spark your imagination, and inspire you. Wherever you are and whatever you do I wish you safe, fun, and inspiring travel.

Lisa Rusczyk Ed. D.
CZYK Publishing

*"A man who can dominate a
London dinner-table can dominate
the world."*

– Oscar Wilde.

As a wondrous soul, London is the perfect place to feel both up and n the road, and settled down. It's ever-evolving and continually diversifying, a place where part of the culture is to experience other cultures. Something I will talk about passionately through this book.

For as long as I have lived here in London, there are still endless things that I have not done that I wish to do. There are museums I have not yet explored, quirky areas I have failed to grace with my presence, and restaurants upon restaurants that I have only planned to indulge in. I try new things more often than most, but still find my 'to-do' list rapidly growing. This is what I believe to be one of the most beautiful things about living in London. Here, I laugh in the face of boredom.

I also believe that a hugely important part of most cultures is their food. Cuisines are passed down from generations, honored in preparations and practices and in some cases even used as tools to adhere to beliefs and traditions. Food often represents way more than the food itself; more than a means of survival or a form of entertainment. Granted, I use it solely as both of those things and therefore will use my expertise to offer tips that predominantly talk about the most satisfying tastes and experiences around London.

I hope you will find these tips useful and learn to love London, and food as much as I do, should you not already.

London
United Kingdom

London Climate

	High	Low
January	48	40
February	49	40
March	53	42
April	59	45
May	65	51
June	70	56
July	74	59
August	73	59
September	67	55
October	60	50
November	53	45
December	48	40

GreaterThanaTourist.com

Temperatures are in Fahrenheit degrees.
Source: NOAA

1. TRAVELLING TASTE BUDS

I thought I'd start with some of the more practical tips. London is a very big city, and for non-locals it can be quite overwhelming. But don't worry; the tube is your friend! As long as you're able to read and/or see colors, you'll be able to master the art of changing lines; although, even if you're unable to do either of those things, London Underground does offer assistance facilities where staff can help you on your way.

Signposted as well as it is, and with easily accessible maps and guidebooks there genuinely is no excuse to get lost, even during long walks between interchanges. I mean, sometimes it genuinely feels as though you could have walked to your actual destination faster. There are also buses running twenty four hours, seven days a week to and from the centre of London.

You can use your contactless bankcards and other contactless methods for travel. However, if you wish to take a little souveneer away with you then I could recommend purchasing an Oyster card. Sometimes they have cute London-related pictures on them too to add to the experience. Additionally regarding travel, there is Uber, traditional black cabs and rent-a-bikes. You can even rent bikes that you quite literally pick up and put down all around the city. They're called Santander bikes and are available for as little as £2.

Downloading the Transport for London (TFL) app or visiting their website will help you to plan your journeys and keep you up to speed on any disruptions or closures, which is very helpful on weekends and bank holidays where typically engineering works take place.

Having said that, I believe that sometimes there's something beautiful about getting lost.

2.   THE WAY TO PAY

EVERYWHERE takes credit and debit cards! That is genuinely not an exaggeration. By cards, I should specify that in fact I refer to all forms of electronic payments – phones, watches, any sort of high-tech, new-age, dangerously easy way to spend money you have and wish to utilize. Just when you arrive somewhere you think may not take card payments there they are with their little machines, whether it be a market stall or a kiosk, or an independent café. Card is cool.

3. TIPS ABOUT TIPS

The general consensus is that you leave them. I don't mean leave them out and don't give them. I mean leave a tip. Often a 12% surcharge will be placed on a bill but they are completely discretionary. I would suggest, as with anywhere that if your service and or food and or general experience is terrible then of course don't leave a tip. Ironically, given tip number two about electronic payments, I believe it's always nice to have a little bit of change to give should the surcharge not be there, or you believe someone specific has done an exceptional job and deserves the tip, or at least a separate one personally. A few quid per person (great British pounds) on top of 10-12% is a nice gesture of appreciation. Although unlike some other countries, our waiters and waitresses aren't solely relying on your gratitude to earn a living, so the pressure is off.

4. READ REVIEWS

As helpful as I expect my tips about the eateries themselves to be, I would always advise you to read reviews too. I appreciate that a lot of it is a matter of opinion and often needs to be sprinkled with a pinch of salt, but having a wider scope will help you to choose what's best for you. There are a vast amount of ways and websites to do so. Take a few minutes to skim through ratings, pros and cons, and 'need to knows' before potentially traipsing half way across the city to find that a restaurant isn't child-friendly, or has a live saxophone player when in fact you find the saxophone to be the most annoying musical instrument in the world.

A great way to have a gander at what people think is social media. There are people 'doing it for the gram', pinpointing their locations and sharing pictures accompanied by captions that are giving other potential customers an insight into what the food looks and tastes like, and how much #fun they're having.

5. TIMING IS EVERYTHING

I guess the time you choose really will depend on your personal preference and of course your availability. But there are certainly times public transport, the streets, and of course eateries get particularly busy. If you love the hustle and bustle and are dead set on getting in with the local work-scene, then lunch between 12-2 and dinner between 5-8 will be your thing. But prepare yourself for sardine-like tube rides, weaving in and out of human traffic, and spending more time in the queue than you do at your table. They aren't called peak-times for no reason.

6. MAKE THE MOST OF HAPPY HOUR(S)

Catering to such a vast amount of people, London not only has places that strategically co-exist with one another, maneuvering their happy hours to share customers, but to gain more clientele, often places extend their happy hours. There are literally happy hours that go from 4pm-9pm, or even sometimes all day on specific days. Although typically for drinks, they sometimes include food deals too, so keep your

17

eyes peels for the happiest times to visit restaurants of your choosing.

7. THE MOST IMPORTANT MEAL OF THE DAY

Yes, you guessed it: breakfast. If you're anything like me, as soon as you open your eyes you're already thinking about food as far away as supper. The idea of an English breakfast probably gives you the impression that we all eat in greasy cafes, with red and white checked table cloths and drink black filtered coffee. Well, we do...

There's nothing better than the gut wrenching smell of a fry-up on a hung-over Sunday morning. The more authentic experiences tend to be in the cafes that don't provide alternative milks, or even know what chai seeds are; they stick to the basics, full English, the novelty vegetarian, and omlettes, with chips. Because who wouldn't want chips with their breakfast? (Chips =fries).

On the other hand, If chai seeds and alternative milks are your thing and you're looking for something a little more fancy, there are plenty of quaint places to enjoy poached eggs and hollandaise sauce, or oatmeal alongside a caffe macchiato. Next to an exceptionally posh barbershop in Holborn, The Black Penny is a great choice for this.

However my favorite café is simultaneously more and less than the aforementioned. OZ Café in King's Cross has underwhelming décor and doesn't omit any sort of cozy feeling. However, it doesn't need anything other than its delicious high-quality food and friendly and efficient staff to keep myself, and even the odd local B-list celebrity going back for more. The hash browns are perfectly crisp and the sausage selection is sublime. Reasonably priced for the area, it's my go-to breakfast café choice.

8. THE BEST BRUNCH

Brunch is a pretty big thing in England, and London specializes in popular spots to roll out of bed long after the sun has risen (and by long after I mean they do all day brunch on weekends), and still indulge in your favorite breakfast foods. It really has become somewhat of a culture in London, with women toasting their mimosas on social media, proudly professing to be "women who brunch", and even groups of men indulging in the trend over their poached eggs.

Table Café, an Independent British restaurant just a stone's throw away from Shakespeare's The Globe theatre is a perfect example. They cater for the typical full English, but slightly more posh than the greasy café type, eggs how you want them, but also offer irresistible sweet and savory pancakes and waffles that you'll immediately regret not ordering once you get a glimpse of a stack being delivered to the next table.

Brunch is most definitely an experience than I would recommend that you partake in whilst in London. You'll feel like such a local!

9. DID SOMEONE SAY "BOTTOMLESS"?

Do you know what else a thing is? Bottomless brunch! Often requiring pre-bookings because of their popularity, bottomless brunches are a brilliant excuse to drink at what usually constitutes as an unreasonable time. Mostly on weekends offering prosecco and bloody Marys, you know breakfast-y drinks in a usually two hour time slot.

However, Jones and Sons located in the quirky area of Dalston offers both bottomless drink AND bottomless food. The thing I like most about Jones and Sons is that their service and quality don't suffer for the mass amounts of orders and both their food and drink menus are pretty extensive for the offer. So if you're going to brunch, and you fancy a tipple to go with it, bottomless brunch is the experience for you.

10. LOVE THE LUNCH HOUR RUSH

You can usually tell that it's lunch time without looking at your watch in London. This is because the streets tend to become filled with ravenous worker-bees on a strictly timed lunch break, mostly spent dodging the other worker-bees and standing in queues for food. It's not ideal, but there is something that I love about the lunch rush. There are cons to rush-hour eating that I touched on a little earlier but, the buzz can be exciting.

Lunch time is a lot calmer on weekends, and there are a few corners of the city it can best be enjoyed. There are parks and squares and canals. Admittedly, great for all meals, but atmospherically perfect for a spot of lunch, Barge House is my top pick. Situated along the canal in Hackney, Barge House has an unbeatable laid back atmosphere and puts real heart into their food. Their consistently colorful menu changes seasonally, keeping locals on their toes. And their freshly squeezed juices are not to be missed.

11. AFTERNOON TEA IS TOTALLY A BRITISH THING TO DO

What a delightfully British experience! So delightful that it's common to receive the experience as a gift. There are many themes to choose from around London, rising in popularity: hovering not too far behind the brunch fad. The ultimate experience in my opinion and that of many others I'm sure, has to be Mad Hatters Afternoon Tea. Of course inspired by Alice in Wonderland, Sanderson hotel in Fitzrovia invites you to take a trip down the rabbit hole to indulge in flavorsome cakes, posh filled sandwiches and biscuits (cookies to some). Also scones, exotic fruit juices, and of course tea, all delivered to you in Alice in Wonderland decorated crockery. It's quite pricey, but well worth it for the whimsical experience.

12. BOTTOMLESS AFTERNOON TEA TOO

Someone was going to pitch the idea eventually, right? It is exactly what you're thinking; an unlimited amount of alcohol – usually prosecco or champagne within a time slot, along with traditional treats. Generally these days, the option to add bottomless drinks is slowly but surely creeping onto afternoon tea menus all around the city.

My favorite, by far has to be Afternoon Tea at the Palm Court in Sheraton Grand Hotel. Their luxurious sandwiches are accompanied by freshly-baked scones, and hand crafted sweets that are shaped to adhere to whatever theme or partnership is currently in place; it could be jazz musical instruments, or even tiny hats to replicate those of their Mayfair neighbors Lock & Co Hatters. All of this is enjoyed with free-flowing bubbles in beautiful decorated dinging area, often accompanied by some sort of subtle live musician.

But be careful, sandwiches and scones might be filled with carbohydrates, but the portions of a quaint afternoon tea may not necessarily be enough to soak up two hours worth of unlimited alcohol.

13. SOAK IN A SUPPER TIME VIBES

London is vibrant around the clock. It isn't abnormal for people to eat later in the evenings, or to grab a bite to eat once their night of entertainment has ended. In addition to street-side stalls and your standard kebab shop, many restaurants remain open until late. Bob Bob Ricard is the best supper spot. It is chic and elegant but doesn't give off a snobbish vibe. It has Russian, French, and British cuisines and comes with a "press for champagne" button; be careful of this should you visit post-cocktails. It remains open until midnight on weekends, and until 1am on weekends.

14. INDULGE UNTIL SUNRISE

It is popular in British culture to eat, drunkenly after a night on the town. Now that I'm highlighting this, I'm wondering how any of us stay healthy!

Typically that involves kebabs, pizzas and cheesy chips (hot French fries topped with cheese that becomes melted and delicious); for me however, I prefer it to end a little differently. Anyone familiar with Brick Lane (an area I'll touch on later on), a famous street in Shoreditch knows that the best thing to eat after a night out is a Bagel from Beigel Bake. Their straightforward menu offers traditional bagel fillings such as salted beef and salmon and cream cheese. However, it never quite tastes the same as any bagel you've ever eaten before. It is no wonder that the place is never quiet, despite being open twenty four hours a day.

We'll talk more about dinners and cuisines later on, but for now I thought we would focus on sort of life choices and dietary requirements.

15. EAT THE MEAT

There are a plethora of excellent steak houses in London; along with all you can eat Brazilian joints, and other meaty restaurants in-between.

Steak is relatively expensive wherever you go in London. You can expect it to be the most expensive thing on any mixed-menus. You can pay big bucks for a fancier restaurant where you're looking at up to £100. But I would say for a decent cut of steak at a specialist restaurant, you're looking at around £30, maybe a little more, maybe a little less.

For something a little more up market, try the Gaucho chain, consistent across all of their restaurants, and ever-growing in popularity. Gaucho is the sort of fancier than average restaurant but not too fancy that you can't afford to go there as a birthday treat.

16. LEAVE THE MEAT

Vegetarian specific restaurants aren't too uncommon in London. They are proudly popping up all over the city, from independent falafel bars to full-blown fine dining restaurants; life choices are being catered too more and more as time moves on.

If you don't like meat, but you do love food, Ethos will be your kind of place. It is a vegetarian buffet restaurant, serving delicious, colorful breakfasts, lunches, and dinners seven days a week. Lunch and dinner is pay-by-weight, so it's totally up to you how much you eat, and of course how much you spend, but be sure to add one (or a few) of their sweet dessert treats; my recommendation, the Naughty Chocolate Cake; it is exactly what it says on the tin.

17. NOT EVEN CHEESE?

Veganism is very much a fast-growing life choice. I see vegan options making their way to food menus all over the city, even in the least likely of restaurants such as American diners or even the odd steak house might throw a novelty vegan pasta option on their menu for good measure – not that I imagine many vegans wanting to actually eat at a steak house but, to each their own.

Back in the trendy area of Hackney (and one in Camden too), there is a place called Temple of Saitan. Sound strange? Well, for those who don't know, Saitan is what vegan "chicken" is made from. This eatery is basically just a chicken shop for vegans that I'm pretty sure are converting meat-eaters day by day. A tasty but simple menu of burgers, fillets, and wings, along with expected sides always leaves a long queue of people out their door. Even for non-vegans it is well worth a try.

18. WHERE TO FIND MORE VEGAN FOOD

Seeing as vegans often still get left out, or are given minimal choice, I thought it would be nice to throw another recommendation on here that I am a regular visitor of. A fabulous restaurant that offers more than one vegan specialty is Mildred's. There are three restaurants dotted around central London (King's Cross, Covent Garden, and Camden). Mildred's offers an eclectic mix of vegan (and the odd vegetarian) options, from curries to burgers to salads. I would absolutely recommend the Sri Lankan curry, genuinely tastier than any I tried in Sri Lanka! Although they seat you pretty close to other customers, it's hard to focus on that whilst you're indulging in a rich vegan peanut butter chocolate brownie.

19. THERE'S SOMETHING FOR RAW

Some people decide on a complete raw diet, consisting mostly of completely raw and non processed foods. Challenging, I know. But Ventra laughs in the face of this challenge! Ventra is a restaurant in bustling Soho, serving up solely plant-based dishes with "your health and happiness in mind." It's both nutritious and delicious.

20. SAY SEE YA TO CELIAC!

Noticeably gluten-free is also on the rise. Maybe having not been recognized before, it seems to be a fairly common diagnosis nowadays. Additionally, no one likes to bloat so many people are simply choosing a lower gluten diet.

Restaurants in London, having to cater to such a vast amount of people are generally in touch with tolerances. Niche excels in catering to this specific intolerance and it's no wonder; it is co-owned by a sufferer of Celiac who decided to create a completely gluten-free menu of British food with a modern twist. It is currently a one of its kind restaurant. Based on the idea of 'gluten-free but you don't even know it', Niche's menu remains hearty and scrumptious. It's a little expensive, but if you're celiac, the price you pay for a good pie and a side of onion rings is totally worth it I'm sure.

21. GO NUTS WITH NO NUTS

There are people with nut allergies so severe that they can't even be around other people eating nuts, so this can be an exceptionally important issue for some. Although not usually a fan of the bigger chains, Bill's is a great choice for allergens. They take the issue extremely seriously, with a thirteen page online guide as to what is in what. This is quite common too – restaurants and chains having allergen menus accessible online, so it might be worth having a look for those pre-visit to any restaurant if you have allergens. Staff in Bills is always ready to drop some knowledge on what you can and cannot eat. Nut allergies are sometimes difficult to cater to, so it's comforting to know a restaurant chain with (currently) nineteen restaurants around London alone are making it easy. For some more formal dining, and tequila if you like, Mestizo is a Mexican restaurant with a plentiful no-nut menu consisting of tapas and salads, desserts and sharing dishes. Easy peasy!

22. LOCAL EATING IS DIFFERENT TO TRADITIONAL EATING

The idea behind this tip to remind you about the vast about of cultures immersed in London. There are of course traditions here, and traditional dishes that I will touch on a bit later on. But London offers the taste of so many different cuisines from all around the world. There are way too many to mention, but I will advise you of some of the more popular ones and of course some of my favorite cuisines and restaurants from around the city.

23. THERE REALLY IS PERFECT PIZZA

Pizza is a difficult thing to compare, based on the fact that it isn't too difficult to get wrong. But I did discover that Homeslice sure do get it right! There are a few dotted around Central London but my favorite is located in Neal's Yard, a quirky backstreet area in Covent Garden, this Homeslice offers pizza to eat, and pizza only; no sides, no salads, not even cutlery. They have pizza and drinks, and that is all you need. They're wood-fire baked and taste as good as the whole place smells. You sit ridiculously close to people, and it's always full to the brim, but you learn not to care as soon as that first bite is taken. The pizzas are huge so one between two usually works. Although the menu is small, it isn't basic. They combine things like pumpkin with broccoli, and beef brisket with celery, and the fusions never disappoint.

Never turn your nose up at the pizza sold by the slice on busy high roads or in popular night-life squares. They're often fresh and tasty and to me, there is something cute about eating off of a paper plate, standing on the street watching the world go by.

24. BARTER ON BRICK LANE

Notoriously known for curry houses, Brick Lane is a seemingly never ending street in Shoreditch. It is filled with bars and boutiques on one end, and overridden with curry houses on the other. My recommendation is Cinnamon; even Prince William has enjoyed a meal there. You'll find people outside their curry houses asking if you'd like to eat there and offering you deals. For example, twenty percent off your bill and a bottle of wine. I am into bartering them down to beat the best deal I have so far. "'X' offered one bottle of wine, I would eat here for two." It hasn't failed me yet.

25. CHOW DOWN IN CHINATOWN

China Town is located in Soho and spans across a number of main and side streets. It is sometimes hard to know whether you're still officially in there, although the plethora of Chinese restaurants can give it away. They're not very competitive. You simply choose from one of very similar menus, go in and eat. Four Seasons is very popular and offers a more extensive menu; it'll take you longer to choose the food than it will to eat it. Although if you want a quick pick, I'd say go for the succulent 'crispy trio', char siu pork, crispy pork, and roast duck. Whatever restaurant choice you make, be sure to walk around a bit; enjoy the vibrant red décor of the streets and soak in the oriental atmosphere.

26. TRY SUSHI, WITH A BIT OF SOMETHING SPECIAL

When you think of sushi you naturally think Japanese, right? It makes sense. Well, Sushisamba is more than just Japanese. Sushisamba is a unique mix of three already unique countries; Japan, Brazil and Peru. Inspired by an early 20s cultural coalition, Sushisamba not only serves three traditional dishes alongside many delicious usual picks, it serves them with carnival-themed décor, with 360 degree views of the City of London. Situated on the 38th and 39th floor with panoramic glass elevators at 110 Bishopsgate, with the highest outdoor dining terrace in Europe, Sushisamba is an eclectic and electric mix not to be missed.

27. THE BEST KEPT SECRET FOR THAI FOOD

This tip is so specific to my person experience and existence. I mean, you can get Thai food all over London. But the only reason I know about this particular magnificent Thai restaurant is because I was an actual full-blown local to its location. Singburi is a family-run establishment on Leytonstone's High Street, East London. Their dishes often look unappetizing, their service is nothing more than existent, and barely might I add, and it's always totally full to the brim with locals. On the other hand, their dishes are authentic, their flavors are extraordinary, and its charm is irrefutable. I miss it dearly and must take a trip back there soon. And so should you.

28. GET DELIGHTFULLY TURKISH

There tend to be areas around London, particularly North London that have Turkish restaurants on every corner. Menus are similar, prices are reasonable, and everything else is sort of average in comparison but tasty none the less. Although there is one particular

Turkish restaurant that stands out for me and that is award winning restaurant, Durum. Durum really does set the standards for Turkish food in London. It's a pretty large space in Finchley Central, with simple but elegant and importantly, spotless décor. It's also reasonably priced and offers large portion sizes of succulent traditional Turkish dishes in the typical form of hot and cold mezes, grills and sides. The experience isn't overwhelming but the food alone is enough to keep us returning over and over, hence why it is often busy in the evenings so worth making a pre-booking.

29. ROAST DINNERS AREN'T JUST FOR SUNDAYS

Roast dinners are a very popular and traditional English dish. They were originally meant to be eaten after church on Sundays hence also being referred to as 'Sunday dinners'. They consist of lots of meat, lots of vegetables and lots of gravy – it's a big dish by nature. Atmospherically they do seem to b enjoyed most on Sundays so I would stick with that day. But don't be ashamed to rebel against convention. Nowadays, it's perfectly normal to see a roast dinner on a pub menu seven days a week.

Blacklock in Soho is a brilliant choice for a true roast dinner experience. They serve massive meat sharing plates and supply you will all of the trimmings. And by all I mean trimmings even most English people didn't know were ever part of a roast dinner. Their spuds are roasted to perfection, their gravy boats are flavorful, and their Yorkshire puddings epitomize the perfect balance between crispy and chewy. Is it Sunday yet?

30. FISH AND CHIPS, THE BEST ENGLISH DISH

I cannot speak for everyone but for me, you can't go wrong with a bit of fish and chips. It is the go-to English meal. The option exists on every local pub menu there is (I dare you to try to find me one that it doesn't) and can be easily enjoyed from local chip-shops, "chippys" as they call them in the North of the country. The best I've tasted has been George's on the infamous Portobello Road, West London. A small and simple fish bar serving up fresh mouthwatering cod that was made even more popular by a glowing review from famous chef, Jamie Oliver. You can take your fish and chips away and wonder the beautiful market stalls and colorful buildings of Portobello Road.

31. MASH IT UP

So you've heard of pie and mash, bangers and mash? They are a couple more from a not very extensive list of traditional English dishes. Again, situated on all local pub menus and are go-to home cooked meals amongst households in England. We're quite touchy about what makes a good pie. But satisfyingly, Cockney's Pie and Mash, which couldn't have a more local name if it tried, as 'cockney' is the name used to refer to someone native to East London. Cockney's is also on Portobello Road (although not in East London) supplies crispy coated, generously filled, unrivaled pies at great prices. Their mash (mashed potato for those of you that may not know) is hit and miss but definitely worth the risk for the scrumptious pies. For the most banging bangers, head to Mother Mash in Soho. They also sell pies, but their unique selection of sausages is what really sets them apart from the rest. Smother all of the above with gravy.

32. 'AVE A BIT OF PUB GRUB

An easy and usually cheap food option is pub grub. Its rare pubs don't have food menus these days. They're very 'samey' no matter where you go, consisting of the above mentioned English dishes, typically along with a burger section, a (usually not great) steak section, and then some bits and bobs such as jacket potatoes, sandwiches and salads. You'll be hard-pressed to find exceptional pub food given that pubs tend to specialize in drinks but, you can be pleasantly surprised. In London, especially around Central London there is quite literally a pub on every corner, and then some in-between. I'd suggest simply finding one you like the look of and give it a go – the vibe will be English and the food will generally be mediocre, but the experience will be very local and very worth it.

33. IF YOU DON'T KNOW WHAT A CHEEKY NANDO'S IS, FIND OUT

Nando's is a Portuguese restaurant chain specializing in chicken. There are Nanod's in other countries, but England boasts its popularity significantly. It is an easy pick restaurant for everyone. Reasonably priced and full of flavor, they genuinely never fail with their consistent food quality and speedy service. So popular they introduced the option for takeaway and released a range of their sauces in supermarkets. If you visit London and don't go to Nando's, you might as well have not come at all.

34. EAT ON THE STREET

Street food is somewhat of a culture in London. With food markets popping up both temporarily and permanently in various areas, locals never seem to be too far away from a lunch time Indian snack box, en route lamb pita bread, or a chunky chocolate brownie to tuck into on the train. Street food stalls are also a great way to indulge in a number of cultures and cuisines under the same, well, not roof, but I think you know what I mean.

35. MUNCH AT A MARKET

Similarly to the street food atmosphere markets are a great place to grab a bite at an independent food stall, although you can do it simultaneously to actually shopping for food produce. You could probably fill up just be taste testing around both the food stalls and the retailers. A splendid place to both buy produce, have something to eat, and enjoy the vibes is the famous Borough market, Southwark. Borough Market is one of the biggest and oldest food retail and food source markets in the city. It is a bit of a must-see place for foodies visiting London I would say.

36. BE WILLING TO WALK FOR A COURSE

With all of these specialist food places, the days of having three courses in one restaurant can be behind us. I mean, there is nothing wrong with finding somewhere fabulous and spending a whole evening having a three course or more meal there. But know that doesn't have to be the case. Should you only be visiting for a short time, and want to make the absolute most of your foodie experience, then being willing to move around will be highly beneficial to this, although I have considered that it might be an oxymoron if you are here for a short time and don't want have much to spare. However, in some areas that houses many restaurants such as Soho and Convent Garden you can grab a starter one place, a main meal elsewhere, and then indulge in a dessert somewhere else. From the days beginning to its end, you have probably already identified the fact that you can have about seven different meal times exploring different restaurants. Split the courses up and you could have visited ten places in a day. I appreciate that you would probably be sickeningly full and extremely exhausted but, I think you get the idea.

37. IT'S FINE TO DINE

Rich in culture, but also in wealth, it isn't hard to believe that there are fine dining and Michelin star restaurants all over the city. As I write this there are currently sixty nine Michelin star restaurants in London, ranging from one to three stars. The famous Gordon Ramsey restaurant has maintained three stars since 2001. These types of restaurants are generally not ones that you simply stumble upon, you have to be looking for them and of course making bookings pretty far in advance in most cases. Some of the finest restaurants are situated in luxurious hotels, such as The Goring Dining Room in The Edwardian and

Alain Ducasse at The Dorchester. Choosing restaurants of this caliber is quite obviously an expensive experience. However, in a lot of cases for tourists and locals alike, a well-worth one-in-a-lifetime experience.

38. THERE IS ALWAYS ROOM FOR DESERT

It's probably not too hard to believe that in a big city like London there is plenty of space for restaurants that specialize specifically in deserts, right? Well there are! There are tones of them. There are ice-cream parlors, bakeries, and waffle houses popping up left, right, and centre And I'm not just talking about restaurants that specialize in desert, I'm talking about restaurants that specialize in specialist deserts; dairy-free, sugar-free, specific food Nationalities. So whilst you're enjoying your dinner and naturally thinking 'what's next?' consider that there could be a glorious desert restaurant nearby. Let's talk more about deserts because, well, it's my favorite subject.

39. GET YOUR CHOC ON

To my fellow chocolate lovers you'll be so grateful for this tip! Choccywoccydoodah is the genuine name of the desert restaurant that I am about to pay homage to. Can you guess what their specialty is? Chocolate is like a form of art to Choccywoccydoodah (just a small side note, I laugh aloud every time I type its name). They create amazing shapes and even more amazing cakes in their colorful boutique shop in the heart of the city. It is a place to visit for the truest of chocoholics.

40. SCREAM FOR ICE CREAM

I appreciate that ice cream may not necessarily be the first thing that springs to mind when thinking about eating in London, you know given the typical British weather forecast. But it can be enjoyed none the less. There are many ice creams parlous around London, including chains such as Ben and Jerry's and Haagen-Dazs. For me the best place to get ice cream has to be Gelupo in Soho. An Italian gelateria (no surprise there), serving up freshly made ice cream from an ever-changing menu, introducing new and innovative flavors such as blood orange and ricotta sour cheery. Accompany your ice cream with a delicious hot chocolate and grab some freshly made truffles for the road. You won't regret it.

41. HOLD THE CREAM

So for those of you who are anti-dairy for whatever reason, there is a wonderful place called Yorica that specializes in free-from treats. From ice-cream and cakes, to free-from crepes and waffles, Yorica caters to all of the food intolerances and life decisions. Expelling all fourteen major allergens from their recipes, they're really not playing around when it comes to the idea of free-from, and the best part is that it doesn't reflect in the taste at all. The ice cream is still creamy, their shakes are thick and their crepes are sweet as nuts (but don't contain nuts).

42. IT DOESN'T HAVE TO BE YOUR BIRTHDAY FOR YOU TO EAT CAKE

There are so many amazing bakeries and patisseries in London that a little snack can sometimes turn into a massive sugar rush. There a couple of places that spring to mind when I think of cake. One of which is Hummingbird Bakery; rich and authentic American cakes with bright colors and lasting after tastes supplied in a number of locations around London. All of their locations have a similar, cutesy feel with small seating areas that kind of encourage take-away but can be enjoyed with a quick coffee.

Another cake shop that I highly recommend is Peggy Porschen, let's call it Peggy's for short. Peggy's was voted 'the best cupcakes in the world' by Vanity Fare and that doesn't surprise me at all. In addition to all of Peggy's parlors being absolutely gorgeous to look at, with quaint décor that look as though they were created by somebody who was an actual unicorn in a former life, their cakes are divine. They're immaculate and pristine, so much so you barely want to bite into them. But trust me, you won't be able to resist.

43. THERE DOESN'T HAVE TO BE A SUGAR RUSH EITHER

I appreciate that to some of you may think that I'm not making dessert seem very exciting here but, there are some of you that will truly appreciate this tip, I'm sure! So, there is a bakery in Islington, well two actually called Romeo's. Romeo's is completely sugar-free. They have all the usual; cheesecakes, tarts, pies, they just have them all without sugar. I can genuinely assure you that it has no detriment on the taste of these deliciously sweet desserts. But if you're watching your weight, or you don't want your kids to be running around like headless chickens post-cake then Romeo's could very well be the perfect place for you.

44. GO UP AT THE SHARD

You must have heard about The Shard; the ninety five story sky scraper designed by Italian architect Renzo Piano? Yes, that one. There are a handful of places to eat up at The Shard. This tip isn't necessarily about which one to eat in. It is more about the experience of going up there. The views are unrivaled in London and you can even move from one bar/restaurant to another to allow yourself the full panoramic viewing of the city. Overlooking all of the most beautiful and famous structures; Tower Bridge, Tower of London, and Big Ben, as well as the

London Eye, London Bridge, and River Thames, the views are surreal and truly not to be missed. It doesn't cost anything to go up, just be aware of dress codes in some of the establishments and enjoy one of the best city views in the world.

45. PARTICIPATE IN A THEME

Another thing that London offers all around the city are themed dining experiences. Eating is taken to the next level, and in some cases in becoming less about the food than it is about the experience as a whole. Or in some cases, experiences are used to highlight the food or specific types of food, which will hopefully become clearer as I give more tips about themes. My point is, as well as eating, dining can be a whole fun activity in itself.

46. DINE IN THE DARK

Admittedly, it doesn't necessarily sound like a lot of fun. But this sensory experience is designed to act as an eye opener (no pun intended) aimed to change any preconceived views you may have about the world.

Dans Le Noir offers the opportunity to dine in complete darkness whilst being served by waiters and waitresses that are visually impaired. Albeit all sounds very serious but it truly is a unique way to dine and socialize. And with sharpened sensors you can really taste the food, which hasn't been overlooked or isn't overwhelmed by the settings.

47. DINE WITH BRITISH TV LEGENDS

They won't be the actual legends themselves, but they will be characters playing TV legends. 'Interactive Theatre International, an Australian company invites people to a Faulty Towers dining experience. Faulty Towers was a British TV show broadcast and very popular in the 1970s. Fantastic actors play a few of its characters, Basil and Sybil Towers, and their Spanish waiter Manuel and interact with guests during their meals, inflicting mayhem and provoking laughter from start to finish.

Another is 'Only Fools, the (cushty) Dining Experience' presented to you by the Nags Head, a

49

public house in Peckham. Actors playing a number of popular characters from Only Fools and Horses, an extremely popular British sitcom that aired right across the 1980s riddle you with mischief whilst you indulge in classic pub grub. Delboy and Rodney create immense fun in a laid back and typically-'cockney' environment.

48. ATTEND A MEDIEVAL BANQUET

Exactly as it sounds; King Henry VIII and his royal banquet take you back to the times of knights and jesters, and Kings and Queens. The banquet itself consists on freshly prepared meals that are more than just 'food to go with your entertainment'. Food is served whilst the entertainers sing and dance and immerse you in a night of fantasy.

You can join in, not so much with the likes of jesting and acrobatics, but you can dance with dragons (this probably goes without saying but – not real ones) and even hire costumes in order to get the full feel of the magical medieval experience.

49. TAKE A TRIP ALONG THE SILK ROUTE

Inspired by the legendary travels of Marco Polo, 'Dinner Time Stories' offers a truly unique and innovative experience the uses 3D visual technology and tells the story of his journey across the regions of the silk route. It is a two hour experience that's concept is based around "Le Petit Chef" and his culinary exploits. There and props and decorations and music, and it all changes with each turning of the page into a new chapter. It is essentially one big, two hour, 3D story that you're both listening to and immersed in as you indulge in a six course meal. It's pricy, but if it's your type of thing it is worth forking out. Get it?

50. BE OPEN TO ANY OR ALL OF THE ABOVE

Some of these tips and recommendations may seem completely foreign to some of you (although I guess to some degree, that's the point), but diving head first into the multi-faceted London culture, with your minds open and your taste buds tingling may very well turn out to be the best experiences, and food of your life. It is a large and wondrous city; don't be overwhelmed by its quirks, it's all part of the charm.

BONUS TIPS: CHIN CHIN

I appreciate that I may very well have already highlighted   the fact that Londoners, as a culture generally enjoy an alcoholic beverage. So I thought I would take a little extra time to add some tips about the best places to experience the drinking culture; including some of the city's best drinking areas, bars, and best kept secrets.

1.   GO TO SOHO

Soho is a central area in London filled with an eclectic mix of bars, restaurants, and shops. It houses the iconic Liberty department store, the infamous Carnaby Street, and Oxford and Regret Street shopping districts. Once you've done a spot of shopping you can rest your tootsies in one of countless bars in the area, or continue with the exploration by hopping from one to the next. Or you could do both within the same vicinity; try Six

Stories. It is quite literally a six story bar, each floor as plush and cozy as the next.

2. ENTERTAIN YOURSELF IN COVENT GARDEN

You must have heard of Covent Garden! It is West End's main entertainment area with theatres galore and home to the Apple Market and the Royal Opera House. The bars have pre-show deals, and you can watch buskers on the street from the balconies of the bars. Covent Garden is always buzzing and there are plenty of indoor and outdoor places to choose from. For beer lovers, try Porterhouse. It is a large pub split over three levels that sell hand crafter beer shipped over from Dublin, Ireland. Their international selection is immense and despite this pub being dedicated to drink, I must say, it is one of the ones with delightfully surprising food too.

3. FOR A DOWN-TO-EARTH VIBE, CHECK OUT BRIXTON

Brixton is a laid back multicultural area that brings people from all over the city whom all have the same agenda. We go there to enjoy the casual, chilled atmosphere. Brixton Market, a must-see in itself is surrounded by cocktail bars and comfy boozers. Try Barrio for some funky fresh Latin American vibes that can be enjoyed on some unique and colorful furniture inside, or on their lovely patio outside.

4. HEAD EAST TO SHOREDITCH

If you're looking for trendy, definitely head to Shoreditch. It is one of those 'places to be' types of area. You could go there first thing in the morning and still be enjoying yourself as the sun comes up. It is riddled with bars and continuous entertainment. There are high-end bars, alongside dingy side door bars that seat you on wooden school-type chairs; all equally enjoyable for the atmosphere.

I recall a time in my life where every Sunday was spent with my hands in the air (like I just don't care) in 93 Feet East. There are disco balls, palm trees and a rooftop hideout. It is perfect for summer time vibes. In fact, the entire area of Shoreditch is exceptionally vibrant in the summer. The local park fills up with Frisbee throwers and the bar terraces fill with plastic cups and laugher. It is much better when the outdoorsy side of it can be experienced, but generally busy and enjoyable all year round.

5. REVEAL THE SECRETS

Ever heard of a speakeasy? For those who haven't, speakeasies, also referred to as a blind tiger or a blind pig were establishments selling alcohol against the law during the prohibition in the 1920s and 1930s. They phased out after this period. But today speakeasies are somewhat secret bars that use retro themes and password protection.

London has a number of speakeasies around the city. Some are more well-known than others, such as Cahoots, an underground tube-themed cocktails bar in Soho, and Mr. Fogg's Residence, and around-the-world-in-eighty-days themed bar in Mayfair. Despite their lack of secrecy, both bars have snide entrances and a sort secret feel about them none the less.

Many different themes exist for speakeasies in London, and if you know what you're searching for they're not too difficult to find. They're certainly not cheap and you could end up walking through a sex shop or a refrigerator to get to them but, they're very much worth the price to get 'in the know'.

6. ENJOY THE COOLNESS OF CLERKENWELL

Clerkenwell is another exceptionally trendy area in East Central that houses old industrial warehouses now filled with new flats and creative companies. It's an area that pretty much caters to anyone and everyone. There are independent boutiques, stylish bars, and cozy gastro pubs. Workers dominate the day times and younger people flock there to enjoy the nightlife. If you're into cabaret, check out Hester's Hideout, a hip bar serving a concoction of cocktails whilst keeping burlesque alive in the basement (that probably sounded more disturbing than intended).

7. LOCK YOURSELF AWAY IN CAMDEN

Swarming with the alternative; alternative music, food, people, Camden is a counter-culture haven that invites everyone to come together to eat and drink, shop and exist without judgment. Camden is both thriving in the day time and thriving in the night time.

People from all walks of life gather on Camden Lock around Regents Canal. Not for the faint-hearted, Camden can get exceptionally busy, especially on weekends so prepare for the dodging of human traffic.

For a less 'punky', more sophisticated experience of Camden, try The Jazz Café. Homegrown talent, and stars from all over the world come to play soul and reggae in this famous, intimate venue. Dance and drink the day and night away in one of the liveliest areas in the city.

8. GET A TASTE OF ITALY IN LITTLE VENICE

Genuine named Little Venice, this area located in Paddington is exactly how it sounds. It is a beautiful neighborhood situated right where the Grand Union Canal and Regents Canal meet. It's bursting with canal boats and beaming with bright white terrace townhouses. One of the most aesthetically pleasing areas in London in my opinion (although kind of ironically resembling a completely different city in a whole other country), it is the perfect place for a glass of Italian wine in a waterside cafe, or a cold beer in one of a handful of floating restaurants.

You can take an actual boat trip along the canal if you wish, or stay still and watch the water pass you by. It gets busier during weekdays as the evening draws near, but there remains something calming about the area throughout.

9. DIG DEEP INTO YOUR POCKETS AND DRINK IN STYLE

For a classier treat, head to Chelsea. If you know anything about London, just reading the name of the area would have taken your mind to the idea of a fancy, shall we say glossier experience? There certainly isn't anything wrong with a good old dive bar, but from time to time it's nice for a more up market treat. If you're willing and able, try some of Chelsea's flashy establishments.

Some places are members only, or at least have member's only sections, and there are quite a few speakeasies (remember those?) in the area too, but generally as long as you dress accordingly you'll be able to flaunt into a number of glamorous cocktail bars where champagne is treated like tap water and the atmosphere is borderline intimidating.

10. GIVE A BIG HAND TO CLAPHAM

Spread across two boroughs of South West London, Clapham is a great all-rounder area for drinking, eating and being entertained. Clapham Common is the heart of the area. It is a lively recreational area that often attracts groups of friends with bags of beer to relax on sunny days. There are pubs that surround the common and allow you to enjoy its beauty and engage in some always fun (in my opinion) people watching. There beer gardens, late-night cocktail joints, and quirky wine bars. Like I said, it's a great all-rounder.

TOP REASONS TO BOOK THIS TRIP

1.   Culture: I have travelled all around the world and visited many major cities including Tokyo, New York and Sydney. But for me, London is by far the most diverse, multi-cultured and vibrant cities of them all. People visit and live here from all over the world, leaving a beautiful mix of race, heritage and general diversity across the city.

There are a plethora of museums and art galleries to be enjoyed, some of which give an insight into the culture and history of London and Britain, such as The Museum of London in St Paul's, and Take Galleries that exhibits a large collection of British art.

Famous landmarks like Big Ben and Buckingham Palace, as well The Royal Family themselves draw millions of tourists per year, admiring London's traditions and heritage. Icons such as red telephone boxes and black taxi cabs are novelties that bring joy to those lucky enough to visit what is understandably believed to be the culture capital of the world.

2.   Entertainment: London is renowned for housing some of the best venues for an array of performance types. The West End theatre district houses endless shows every night of the week, bringing the biggest names in the industry to perform on our stages.

Music festivals are ever growing in quality and quantity. Carnivals and Concert Halls bring acts and listeners from all over the world. One million people pay homage to Caribbean culture every year at Notting Hill Carnival. The O2 Arena holds twenty thousand screaming fans, whilst Ronnie Scotts holds an intimate two hundred and fifty people who can enjoy some of the biggest jazz musicians in the world.

There are man-made beaches in the summer, Wonderlands in the winter, and pop up parties all year round. You can find anything from comedy shows, open mic nights and cinemas, to ballet, opera and drag shows daily, all right at your fingertips. It's also easy to source out free shows where newcomers can showcase their talents and you get reap the benefits of the aspiration of an artist.

London's wonder feels infinitive. There truly isn't an excuse to ever be bored in a city so big, so beautiful, and so buzzing.

3.   Beauty: I haven't been able to touch too much on the aesthetics of London as a city. So I guess now is my chance; what a gorgeous place it is!

Architecturally London never ceases to astound me. There is an amazing contrast between the old and new allowing you to discover historic churches and palaces, as well as metropolitan areas dominated by shiny skyscrapers.

Its beauty is often overlooked by locals, but despite the concept of this book I certainly wouldn't advise you to do the same. Around any given corner there could be a beautiful monument, statue, or sculpture. London offers an endless supply of parks, commons, and greens. Richmond Park boasts over two thousand acres of beauty, whilst Bushy Park follows with over one thousand. The popularity of Hyde Park and Regents Park is continual and Nature Reserves and Woodlands are scattered throughout the city.

There are hills and viewpoints such as Alexandra Palace and Primrose Hill where you can watch as the sun set shifts from the day buzz to the night.

The River Themes runs gloriously through the city, as does the fourteen kilometer Regent's Canal. There are locks, lakes, and ponds, well as waterfalls, fountains, and reflecting pools.

When it comes to the beauty that London has to offer, there truly is too much to mention. You have to come to see it for yourself. I guess that's the real beauty of it.

"I've been walking about London for the last 30 years, and I find something fresh in it every day"

– Walter Besant.

OTHER RESOURCES:

www.tfl.co.uk – For travel updates

www.tripadvisor.co.uk – For customer reviews

www.timeout.com – For entertainment

READ OTHER CZYK PUBLISHING BOOKS

Greater Than a Tourist- St. Croix US Birgin Islands USA: 50 Travel Tips from a Local by Tracy Birdsall

Greater Than a Tourist- Toulouse France: 50 Travel Tips from a Local by Alix Barnaud

Children's Book: *Charlie the Cavalier Travels the World* by Lisa Rusczyk

Eat Like a Local

Follow *Eat Like a Local on* Amazon.

METRIC CONVERSIONS

TEMPERATURE

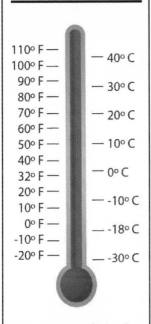

110° F — — 40° C
100° F —
90° F — — 30° C
80° F —
70° F — — 20° C
60° F —
50° F — — 10° C
40° F —
32° F — — 0° C
20° F —
10° F — — -10° C
0° F —
-10° F — — -18° C
-20° F — — -30° C

To convert F to C:

Subtract 32, and then multiply by 5/9 or .5555.

To Convert C to F:

Multiply by 1.8 and then add 32.

32F = 0C

LIQUID VOLUME

To Convert:..................Multiply by
U.S. Gallons to Liters................ 3.8
U.S. Liters to Gallons 26
Imperial Gallons to U.S. Gallons 1.2
Imperial Gallons to Liters....... 4.55
Liters to Imperial Gallons 22
1 Liter = .26 U.S. Gallon
1 U.S. Gallon = 3.8 Liters

DISTANCE

To convert ....Multiply by
Inches to Centimeters 2.54
Centimeters to Inches 39
Feet to Meters...................... .3
Meters to Feet 3.28
Yards to Meters 91
Meters to Yards 1.09
Miles to Kilometers 1.61
Kilometers to Miles............ .62
1 Mile = 1.6 km
1 km = .62 Miles

WEIGHT

1 Ounce = .28 Grams
1 Pound = .4555 Kilograms
1 Gram = .04 Ounce
1 Kilogram = 2.2 Pounds

Manufactured by Amazon.ca
Bolton, ON

19636836R00049